Hotel Room Trilogy

D1430192

TRICKS

BLACKOUT

MRS. KASHFI

Barry Gifford

University Press of Mississippi
Jackson

HOTEL ROOM

TRILOGY

The first hardcover edition of *Hotel Room Trilogy* is limited to five hundred copies signed by the author.

Copyright © 1995 by Barry Gifford
All rights reserved
Manufactured in the United States of America

98   97   96   95   4   3   2   1

The paper in this book meets the guidelines for permanence and durability of the Committee on Production Guidelines for Book Longevity of the Council on Library Resources.

CAUTION: These plays are fully protected in whole, in part, or in any form, under the Copyright Laws of the United States of America, the British Empire, including the Dominion of Canada, and all other countries of the Copyright Union, and are subject to royalty. All rights, including professional, amateur, motion picture, recitation, radio, television, and public reading are strictly reserved. All inquiries should be addressed to the author's agent: Matthew Snyder, Creative Artists Agency, 9830 Wilshire Boulevard, Beverly Hills, CA 90212-1825.

Library of Congress Cataloging-in-Publication Data
Gifford, Barry, 1946–
    Hotel room trilogy / Barry Gifford.
      p.   cm.
    Contents: Tricks.—Blackout.—Mrs. Kashfi.
    ISBN 0-87805-776-5.—ISBN 0-87805-777-3 (pbk.)
    1. Hotels—Drama.   I. Title.
PS3557.I283H68   1995
812'.54—dc20   94-23776
                                       CIP

British Library Cataloging-in-Publication data available

This book is dedicated to
Daniel Schmid and Jane Birkin
for Taormina

Contents

Preface

These plays were commissioned by David Lynch and Monty Montgomery, executive producers of the Home Box Office television series *Hotel Room. Tricks* and *Blackout* were directed by Mr. Lynch and shown as two of three pilot programs in 1993. The only rules regarding composition were that the action take place in specific years—*Tricks,* for example, is set in 1969—and be set in a particular New York City hotel room (numbered 603), the corridor immediately outside the room, and the hotel lobby. A bellboy and maid, the only continuing characters in the series, were to be included in the plays at my option.

Mrs. Kashfi, modelled after an early short story of mine of the same title, is based on experiences I endured as a child when I accompanied my mother on her uncharted voyages into the sea of clairvoyance. *Tricks* was begun in New Orleans while I was covering the Louisiana gubernatorial race between former Ku Klux Klan leader David Duke and Edwin Edwards for the Spanish newspaper *El País. Blackout* was written in two days with the admonition from Messrs. Montgomery and Lynch that it be "something our grandmothers could watch." I told Monty that would not be a problem; I'll write the play, I said, you guys gag and tie up the old ladies.

—B.G.
Chez Carothers
Lawrence, Kansas, June 1993

P.S. Thanks to Harry Dean Stanton, Freddie Jones, Glenne Headly, Alicia Witt and Crispin Glover, for so brilliantly bringing various of these characters to life. And very special thanks to David Lynch, for his perfect direction.

Hotel Room Trilogy

TRICKS

Characters

BOCA, *a middle-aged man*

LOU, *another middle-aged man*

DARLENE, *a young prostitute*

BELLBOY

MAID

TWO PLAINCLOTHES COPS

SETTING: *a hotel room in New York City, 1969*

NOTE: *The pace of the play is slow but tense, the actors'
movements almost agonizingly exaggerated, their
words deliberate with a kind of mock profundity. The
impression should be one or two steps removed from
reality.*

EMPTY HOTEL CORRIDOR

Elevator door opens. BELLBOY *holds door and* MAN *and* WOMAN *emerge. The* MAN, *who is in early middle age, is conservatively dressed, wearing a business suit. The* WOMAN, *who is a hooker, is much younger, provocatively dressed and heavily made-up. The couple do not touch as they proceed down the hall. They have no bags. The* BELLBOY *hustles ahead of them, room key in hand.*

Bellboy
Here we are, room 603.

BELLBOY opens the door, stands back and allows the couple, the WOMAN *first, to enter the room. The* BELLBOY *follows them inside, turns on lights, etc. The hooker goes over to the window, looks out, remains standing. The* MAN *takes money from his pocket, holds it out to* BELLBOY.

HOTEL ROOM

Man
Thanks, fella. This is for you.

BELLBOY takes tip, hands MAN *the room key.*

Bellboy
Anything you need sent up?

Man
No, no. Not at the moment. I don't think. Wait. Uh, Arlene, you want something? A drink?

Woman
*Dar*lene. My name is *Dar*lene.

Man
Right, Darlene. You need anything?

Darlene

I got what I need.

DARLENE *takes a cigarette from her purse, lights it, smokes.*

Man *(to* BELLBOY*)*

No, fella. I'll call down, we need something.

Bellboy *(as he exits)*

Enjoy yourselves.

The MAN *walks around the room, looking it over.*

Man

Damn! I asked for a double bed, not two singles.

He sits down on one of the beds. He's clearly nervous. DAR-LENE *remains by the window, smoking, not looking at him.*

Man

You need to use the bathroom? There's the bathroom.

DARLENE *does not respond. The* MAN *picks up the phone, which is on the table between the two beds. He dials an extension.*

Man

This is Mr. Boca, in, let's see *(looks at key)*, room 603. Yeah, how about sending up a fifth of Johnnie Walker Black and some ice. Yeah, it's gotta be Black. Okay, okay. Black, yeah, there's a *big* difference. And a couple chimneys. Chimney-size glasses, that's right. Okay, okay. Boca, yes. Ah, ah.

BOCA *hangs up. Stands, sits again. Stands, starts to walk over to* DARLENE, *stops.*

Boca

I gotta go.

Darlene

We just got here.

Boca

I mean to the bathroom. Before the drinks come.

Darlene

You need help, that's why I'm here.

> BOCA *goes into the bathroom, closes the door after him.* DAR-LENE *comes around to where the beds are, puts out her cigarette in an ashtray. She sits down on the bed* BOCA *did not sit on, opens her purse and takes out a plastic bag half-filled with marijuana and some Zig-Zag papers. She proceeds to roll a joint. The toilet in the bathroom flushes and* BOCA *comes out, sees what she's doing.*

Boca

Damn! Is that what I think it is?

Darlene

I don't know you, mister. How do I know what you think?

> BOCA *sits on the bed opposite* DARLENE, *studying her. She lights the joint, takes a drag and holds it out toward* BOCA.

Darlene

Want a hit?

Boca

No! I mean, let me think about it.

Darlene

You think too much, man, is what I think.

> BOCA *stands up, sits down again. Watches her.* DARLENE *inhales deeply on the joint, tilts her head back.* BOCA *slides off his bed onto his knees in front of* DARLENE. *She looks at him.*

Darlene

What are you thinking about now?

Boca

The White Knight is about to undertake a dangerous journey through the dark forest.

Darlene

Far out, man. You're into fairy tales, huh?

> *There is a knock on the door.* BOCA *gets up and opens it, allowing the* BELLBOY *to enter, carrying a tray with a bottle, two tall glasses and a bucket of ice on it.*

Bellboy

Your order, sir.

> *The* BELLBOY *places it on the table, hands a check and a pen to* BOCA.

Bellboy

Sign this, please, sir.

> BOCA *signs the check. The* BELLBOY *sniffs the marijuana smoke, smiles at* DARLENE.

Bellboy

Thank you, sir.

> *The* BELLBOY *starts to leave.*

Boca

Wait!

> BOCA *hands a dollar bill to the* BELLBOY.

Bellboy

Thank you, sir. Enjoy yourself.

> *The* BELLBOY *leaves.* BOCA *pours two stiff drinks, holds a glass out to* DARLENE.

Darlene

You go ahead. I'm fine for now.

> BOCA *sucks down half of the contents of the glass. He pauses, then swallows the rest of it. He stands up and takes off his jacket, hangs it over the back of a chair.*

Darlene

Before the White Knight takes out his sword, he has to pay tribute to the fair maiden.

Boca

Right, sure.

He takes a money clip from a pants pocket, removes some bills and hands them to DARLENE. She takes the money and places it in her purse. She puts the roach into the ashtray, stands up and starts to undress. There is a knock on the door.

Boca

Damn! Who's there?

Voice from Corridor

Lou.

Boca

Lou! What's Lou doing here? Doing here *now.*

Darlene

Who's Lou?

Knock on door again. BOCA opens it. LOU, a man about the same height and age as BOCA, enters the hotel room. He sees DARLENE, smiles. He ignores BOCA, goes over to the table and picks up the second glass. LOU looks DARLENE over, raises the glass to her, then drinks from it.

Boca

Lou! What's this? What are you doing here? Doing here *now!*

Lou

This is something here, Moe. Something you got here.

Boca

You can't, Lou. Just can't, not now.

Lou

Did you pay her, Moe?

Boca

Lou! No!

Lou

Answer me, Moe. Did you pay her yet?

Boca

I paid her.

> LOU *is clearly pleased.* BOCA *is fiercely agitated, sweating, upset.* LOU *finishes the rest of his drink, hands the empty glass to* BOCA, *who takes it.*

Lou

Fix me another, will you?

> LOU *sits down on the bed next to where* DARLENE *is standing.*

Lou

Sit, sweetheart. Sit next to Lou.

> *He pulls her down, gently, next to him.* BOCA *pours* LOU *a drink and another one for himself.* BOCA*'s hand trembles as he hands the glass to* LOU.

Lou

What's your name, baby?

Darlene

Darlene.

Lou

Are you from the city, Darlene? Were you born here?

Darlene

I'm from Iowa. Des Moines, Iowa.

Boca

Lou! Who cares where she was born? This isn't . . . this is *not right!*

Lou

Moe, calm down. Your heart, you know. You know what could happen.

> BOCA *sits down on the other bed.* LOU *returns his attention to* DARLENE.

Lou

I was in Iowa once. It must have been ten, eleven years ago. Driving through with my first wife, Felicia. Our son, Arthur, was born, let's see, in 1960. This was a year or so before Arthur was born. Felicia hated Iowa, I remember. Cornfields. Cornfields all across Iowa in the summer. It was hot and we, we didn't have air-conditioning in the car!

Boca

Lou! Damn you, Lou!

Darlene

Are you guys friends, or what?

> LOU *laughs and* BOCA *stands up, spilling most of his drink on himself.*

Boca

You shouldn't be talking about Felicia, Lou! Not here, not now! It's not right!

Lou

No, it's not, Moe, it's probably not. What should we be talking about, Moe?

Boca

Yesterday I read in a magazine about the movie actress, Martine Mustique. You know who she is, Lou? Martine Mustique? She died a couple of weeks ago, a month before her thirtieth birthday.

Lou

Yeah, sure. The tall, skinny broad with good tits.

Boca

Did you know that she and Felicia had the same birthday, Lou? The fifteenth? Did you know that?

Lou

I don't . . . I don't know if I did or not, Moe.

Boca

Martine Mustique wasn't her real name. It was Rima Dot Duguid, and she was born in North Carolina, or Georgia, some state like that. She was married twice before she turned nineteen. Had a couple abortions. Ran off from there and changed her name to Sarita Something. Sarita Touché, that was it. Turned up in Europe with a Persian art dealer named Darwish Noof. She was spotted on the beach on the French Riviera by the owner of a cosmetics company. That's how she became a model and got to Hollywood. That's where her name got changed again.

Lou

She did those perfume ads, for, what was it called? Parachute?

Boca

Paroxysme, Lou. That's French. *Paroxysme.* She stood on the edge of a cliff wearing a nightgown.

Lou

Oh, yeah. Without no bra.

Boca

She was a big star, Lou, a *real* star. I saw all of her movies. *Forever Ruthless. Lost Among the Living. The Big Ache.*

Lou

That was a good one, Moe. *The Big Ache.* Where she murders a dentist who's been drilling phony cavities.

Boca

Then she was found murdered—decapitated—in the bathtub of her house in the Hollywood hills. A guy she'd thrown over, Edgard Shtup-Louche, the heir to Louche Industries, manufacturers of forty-five varieties of condoms, mailed a confession to the LA police department before hanging himself in a gazebo on the Shtup-Louche estate in Bel-Air. In his letter, Edgard said that Martine had refused his proposal of marriage after forty-eight hours of virtually continuous lovemaking. He said she was the only woman with whom he was able to achieve an erection. When she turned him down, he said, she denied him his only chance for lifelong happiness. Rather than murder all of the psychiatrists who'd attended him since childhood, Edgard said, it was easier just to do away with the object of his affection. And, of course, himself.

Lou
That's tragic, Moe. That's what tragedy can do to a person.

Boca
I saw Martine Mustique's last movie, that came out after her death. *The Brave and the Beautiful.* She played a Croatian lion tamer named the Great Vukovara, a woman torn between her love for her home and family and a Serbian soldier during the Yugoslavian civil war. She learns that her lover has been killed by Croat freedom fighters just before she must stage a command performance for the Queen of England, but she goes on as scheduled, right? At the end of her act, Vukovara tosses aside her whip and chair and orders the lions to attack her. As the big cats tear the Great Vukovara apart, superimposed on the screen is a picture of Martine Mustique at her most beautiful, the way she looked in that ad for *Paroxysme.*

Lou
Jesus.

Boca
Yeah. And you know what she said her biggest regret in life was, Lou? What it said in the magazine article?

Lou

No, Moe. What?

Boca

That she'd never gotten to be a cheerleader in high school. Isn't that too much, Lou?

Darlene

I was a cheerleader in high school there. In Des Moines.

Lou

That couldn't have been very long ago, Darlene. Do you remember how to do them? The cheers?

Boca

Lou, Lou, I'm begging you.

Lou

Darlene, honey. Do one for us. Do one of your high school cheers for us.

Darlene

You really want me to?

Lou

Yes! Absolutely.

> DARLENE *stands up, walks over to the area in front of the bathroom, where there is more space. She kicks off her shoes.*

Darlene

(recites cheer with appropriate accompanying gestures)

California oranges, Texas cactus,
We play your team just for practice!
Give me an R! Give me an O!
Let's go, let's go, let's go!
Give me a C! Give me a K!
Let's kick their butts today!
Give me an E! Give me a T!
Make 'em see, make 'em see, make 'em see!

Give me an S! We're the best!
R-O-C-K-E-T-S! Rockets rule
the whole Midwest!
Rockets! Rockets!
Yaaaaaay, Rockets!

> DARLENE *attempts to do the splits as she completes the cheer and falls over on the floor.* LOU *rushes over and helps her up.*

Darlene
Shit, I'm pretty stoned.

Lou
That was great, baby. Great!

> LOU *fondles* DARLENE *all over and they move toward one of the beds as* BOCA *stands and watches, horrified.*

Boca
Lou, no! Lou!

> *From outside the hotel room window, we watch* LOU *guide* DARLENE *across the room, past* BOCA, *whose protests they ignore completely.* LOU *helps* DARLENE *undress, after which he takes off his own clothes, and they tumble onto one of the beds, out of our sight. We see* BOCA, *who is watching* LOU *and* DARLENE *make love, obviously tormented by their actions.*
>
> *After they have finished,* LOU *and* DARLENE *lie on their backs smoking cigarettes.* BOCA *is sitting on the other bed, a fresh drink in his hand. He is composed now, expressionless.*

Lou
You're all right, baby. You really are. Don't you think so, Moe? Isn't Darlene all right?

Boca
She's all right, Lou.

Lou

No, Moe, I mean it! I mean, she is really all right! It's not every hooker in New York can do a cheer like that, let me tell you.

Darlene

I could have been a cheerleader at the university, too, if I'd gone there. The University of Iowa, I mean.

Lou

Sure you could've.

Darlene

I got pregnant, though, so I didn't. I stayed home and had the baby.

Lou

You left the kid with your mother and followed your boyfriend to New York. He came to be an actor and was working as a bicycle messenger.

Darlene

He didn't want me, though, the bastard. I tried to kill him. Stabbed him four times with a kitchen knife, but he lived.

Lou

If you'd had a gun, you would have shot him.

Darlene

I would. I would have shot him once in each knee, made him crawl like a snake before I delivered the coup de grace.

Lou

Do you mean that, Darlene? You would have done that to your boyfriend?

Boca

Why doubt her, Lou? I don't, I don't believe she would lie about that.

Darlene

I remember in high school, in high school in Des Moines, Iowa, I read in a science class a book about snakes. There was a part in the book about the mating habits of pit vipers, such as rattlesnakes and copperheads. Female copperheads mate only once every three to five years. When one emerges from her den after hibernating for the winter, she's greeted by a whole bunch of male copperheads. These suitors battle one another for the privilege of partaking of her favors. Not by biting, but by wrestling, attempting to force the other down to the ground into a submissive position. This competition can last for hours, or even days. About the same period of time it takes to complete the process of copperhead copulation. Females ignore the weaker male snakes, and even younger males will assert themselves over the defeated adults, whose self-confidence has been severely reduced. Once the competition has been completed, the top snake seeks out the willing female and does it to her.

Lou
Felicia didn't know which end of a gun the bullet comes out of. Isn't that right, Moe? Did she even know how a gun works? Which end to hold, even?

BOCA *shrugs, shakes his head, sips his drink.*

Lou
That's the kind of a woman Felicia was.

Darlene
The female doesn't have a chance. Not with all those males waiting, ready and willing. Willing to fight each other for the privilege. Women don't have a chance. Not with men, anyway. Not the way they are.

Boca
It's the law of nature. Isn't it, Lou?

Lou
Isn't what, Moe?

Boca
The law of nature.

Lou

I suppose, Moe. I suppose it is.

Darlene

Men make the law. Nature's got nothin' to do with it.

Boca *(to* DARLENE*)*

You were gonna blow his brains out, you said.

Lou

She stabbed him, Moe. She said she stabbed him, how many times?

Boca

Four. Four times in a row.

> DARLENE *turns on her side, away from* LOU. *She is crying softly, trying not to let the men see her tears.*
> LOU *gets out of bed and goes into the bathroom. We hear the shower go on.*

Darlene *(to* BOCA*)*

Hand me my things, will you?

> BOCA *picks up* DARLENE'S *clothes off the floor and brings them to her. He walks over to the window and stands there while she dresses.*

Boca

Felicia was a cheerleader, too.

Darlene

Who's Felicia?

Boca

You don't remember. You weren't listening. Arthur's mother. Felicia was Arthur's mother. Driving past the corn-fields of Iowa.

Darlene

Oh, yeah. Lou's first wife, right?

Boca *(highly agitated)*

My wife, you mean. Felicia was my wife, not his. Not Lou's. Lou's never been married. Does Lou strike you as the kind of man a woman like Felicia would marry? That's a joke! Felicia wouldn't look twice at Lou, he knows that.

DARLENE *is standing now. She's almost finished dressing.*

Darlene

I've had some strange tricks, man, but you two guys are *weird.* You got a game goin' I ain't seen before.

Boca *(goes to* DARLENE*)*

Game? What do you mean, a *game?*

She moves away, frightened by BOCA*'s intense reaction.*

Darlene

Look, man, just let me get dressed and get out of here. I don't care what's behind it.

LOU *comes out of the bathroom, a towel around his waist.*

Boca

You hear this, Lou? This bitch, this miserable little whore, thinks this is a game! That's what she called it, Lou, I swear.

Lou

Darlene, when you stabbed your boyfriend, the father of your child, you didn't intend to kill him, did you?

Darlene

I did. I did want to kill him. What difference does it make?

BOCA *and* LOU *stand on either side of* DARLENE.

Boca

Ask her, Lou, Come on, ask her.

Lou

His name, Darlene. What was his name?

Darlene

Whose name? What the fuck are you guys talking about?

Boca

Your boyfriend's name, Darlene. Was it *Arthur?*

Darlene

No. No, it wasn't Arthur. Look, I'm gonna split now. See you guys around.

> DARLENE *goes for the door but* BOCA *and* LOU *rush to stop her. They push her up against the door.*

Lou

I don't think so, Darlene. We don't want you to leave yet.

> *There is a knock on the door.*

Female Voice From Corridor

Maid! Do you want your bed turned down for the evening?

Darlene

Call the cops! These guys are gonna hurt me!

Boca

Damn it, Lou!

> DARLENE *opens the door and runs out of the room, past the startled* MAID, *towards the elevator. The* MAID *stands back, not sure what to do.*

Lou   *(to* MAID)

Don't worry, honey, it's all right. Nothing's wrong.

> LOU *and* MAID *watch* DARLENE *get into the elevator and the elevator door close.* BOCA *hands* LOU *a few bills and* LOU *gives them to the* MAID.

Lou

Here, sweetheart, take this. We don't need the room fixed. Everything's fine.

Maid

You want the bedtime mints?

She holds out two goldfoil-wrapped chocolate mints. LOU *takes them.*

Lou

Thanks, precious.

LOU *goes back inside the room and shuts the door on the* MAID.

Lou

That was close, Moe.

LOU *gets dressed.* BOCA *picks up the bottle of Johnnie Walker Black and sits down on the unused bed. He takes a swig of Scotch straight from the bottle.*

Boca

It could have happened, Lou. You know it could have happened.

Lou

Pass it here, Moe. Pass the bottle.

BOCA *hands the bottle to* LOU, *who takes a drink. He returns the bottle to* BOCA.

Lou

Moe, I'm not sorry. I'm not sorry about any of it. Do you understand?

Boca

Sure, Lou. I understand. I've always understood. Just like you.

Lou

Life goes on, Moe. If you're lucky.

Boca

I felt lucky once. It happened when I was a kid, eleven,

twelve years old. I was delivering Chinese food on a bicycle. A quarter an hour and a dime a delivery, plus tips. The tips were crucial, Lou, crucial.

Lou

I know about crucial, Moe. Tell me about crucial.

Boca

I had a third floor delivery on a Sunday night. It was pissing outside, raining hard while I rode, soaking the brown bags. So I go up the stairs. I can feel the subgum sauce leaking on my hands from the bottom of the bag. A woman opens the door, tells me put the bag down on the kitchen table. This woman, she's wearing a pink nightgown which is half open in front. I could see her nipples through it. Her hair was black halfway down her head, the bottom half bleach blond, kind of stringy.

Lou

Unkempt. She was unkempt.

Boca

Yeah, well, she asks me how much she owes and I say five dollars. I see her cheeks and chin is got purple dust all over. She tells me she'll be right back and goes out of the kitchen. I wait there, look around. There's dirty dishes piled in the sink, one of the elements of the overhead fluorescent light is burned out. The whole kitchen is glowing, rose-colored, like the woman's face and her nightgown.

Lou

You got my interest, Moe.

Boca

The woman comes back and gives me a fifty-dollar bill. Now she has on a green nightgown similar to the one she had on before. She shows me her tongue.

Lou

What do you mean, she shows her tongue?

Boca

Flicks it out, in and out, like a snake.

Lou

Jesus, Moe. You're how old?

Boca

Eleven, twelve. I tell her I don't have change for that big a bill. I ask her if she has anything smaller. She says to wait, she'll go see. She leaves me alone again. I spot bugs.

Lou

Bugs? Where?

Boca

On the sink, crawling on the dishes stacked there.

Lou

Spooky, the way some people live.

Boca

She comes back and I'm disappointed she has on the same green nightgown. She hands me a twenty. Will this do? she asks. I dig in my pocket for change, but she stops me. Puts a hand on my wrist. Keep it all, she says.

Lou

Whoa!

Boca

Yeah. She takes my hand and leads me to the front door, where I came in. Now guess what happened?

Lou

Give it to me.

Boca

She puts my hand on one of her breasts.

Lou

The shit, Moe. The shit.

Boca

She says, thank you, thank you, like in a heavy, deep voice. Like Lauren Bacall or Tallulah Bankhead. She looked like Tallulah Bankhead except for her hair, which was more like Lauren Bacall's.

Lou

What did you do?

Boca

I said, you're welcome.

Lou

That's all?

Boca

Yeah. She opened the door, and I went out, down the stairs. It was still raining, you know? But I stood out there, under a Dutch elm tree where I'd left my bike. Stood in the rain for a few seconds. I put my hand in my pocket and felt to see the twenty-dollar bill was there. I remember thinking, if I could just have two deliveries like this a day, just two.

Lou

Moe, Jesus Christ, Moe. Listen, I'm goin' now. You comin'?

Boca

Not yet.

Lou

Don't wait too long.

Boca

Yeah, okay.

Lou

Remember, don't wait too long.

Boca

Yeah, yeah, I heard you. So long, Lou.

Lou

So long, Moe.

> LOU *goes out.* BOCA *swigs from the bottle.*

Fade Out.

Fade In.   *The hotel room. Night. There is a knock on the door.*

Loud Male Voice From Corridor

Open up! Open up this door!

> BOCA *rouses himself from the bed, where he has drunk himself to sleep. The knocking continues until* BOCA *stumbles over and opens the door. Two* PLAINCLOTHES COPS *enter the room.*

Cop #1

Louis Holchak? Are you Louis Holchak?

Boca

No, no! I'm not!

Cop #2 *(picks up* BOCA'S *jacket)*

This your coat?

Boca

Huh? Maybe. Yeah, yeah, it must be.

> COP #2 *finds wallet in coat, opens it.*

Cop #2

This is Louis Holchak's driver's license. Louis Holchak's credit cards. Louis Holchak's social security card.

Cop #1

If you're not Louis Holchak, what're you doin' with his wallet?

Cop #2

It's him. It's his picture on the license.

Boca

No, look. Lou was just here. He's . . .

Cop #1   *(taking hold of* BOCA*)*

You're under arrest for the murder of Felicia Boca. Anything you say may be held against you as evidence in a court of law. Do you understand?

Boca

I . . . I . . .

Cop #1

Do you understand?

Boca

I . . . yes . . . I mean, no. No, I don't understand! I don't! I don't understand!

Fade Out.

END

BLACKOUT

Characters

DANNY, *a man in his late thirties*

DIANE, *Danny's wife; she is in her mid-thirties.*

BELLBOY

SETTING: *a hotel room in New York City. Mid-summer. [In the original production, the play was set in the year 1936.]*

DARKNESS. WE SEE NOTHING
BUT PITCH BLACK.

We hear voices, feet on stairs. Suddenly, a beam of light coming from a stairwell off what we can barely discern as an empty hotel corridor. Now there are two beams of light streaming into the corridor as the voices grow louder and the steps are more audible. The shapes of two men, both holding flashlights, one of them carrying a bag in one arm, enter the corridor from the stairwell. Their flashlight beams precede them as they turn and walk toward us down the corridor.

Bellboy
Watch out, for the carpet here. The edge of it. Don't get your toe caught under the edge. The toe of your boot, I mean.

Danny   *(Laughs.)*
Thanks, I won't. I been walkin' in boots since I was born, practically.

Bellboy   *(Stops in front of door to room number 603.)*
You're from where? Nebraska?

Danny
No. Oklahoma. My wife and me are from Big Eagle, Oklahoma. Outside Tulsa.

Bellboy
You get blackouts in Big Angle? Electrical blackouts like this?

Danny
Big Eagle. No, not really. Not too many lights to begin with. Not in Big Eagle. Tulsa's a big town, though. Ever been there?

Bellboy
No, sir. Farthest west I've been's Jersey City. That's in New Jersey, just across the Hudson River.

Danny

Do you mind opening the door for me? With this bag of food and the torch, it's tough to get at my key.

Bellboy *(Quickly takes out his master key.)*
Oh, sure, yes sir. Sorry. *(He unlocks the door and stands aside.)* There you are, sir.

> DANNY *enters the room, followed by the* BELLBOY. *Lightning flashes outside the window, followed by a crash of thunder. This continues intermittently throughout.*

Danny

Hey, darlin'. You in here somewhere?

> *Both* DANNY *and the* BELLBOY *wave their flashlights around until they locate* DIANE, *who is sitting on a couch in the dark. The lights circle and blind* DIANE *momentarily. She puts one hand up and covers her eyes.* DANNY *puts the bag down on a table, then switches off his flashlight. He sits next to his wife while the* BELLBOY *begins lighting candles all around the room.*

Danny

Sweetheart, you okay? I got us some Chinese for supper. *Good* Chinese.

Bellboy *(Strategically setting up the candlestick holders.)*
The best. Low Fon's the best around here. New York's got the best Chinese food in the world. Better than in China. At least that's what our Chinese guests tell me. I was never actually in China. But I guess the Chinese should know.

> DANNY *has one arm around* DIANE *as they sit together on the couch. She still has one hand over her eyes. The* BELLBOY *finishes arranging the candles and stands in front of the open room door, holding his flashlight.*

Bellboy

I'm sure they'll get the lights fixed soon. The candles should last until they do. There're more candles in the cabinet there, under the window, if you need 'em. The phones are working—at least they were a few minutes ago. If you need anything else, just call down. I'd recommend, though, that you stay in the room until the power comes on again. New York's not Oklahoma, you know. There're plenty of people take advantage of a situation like this. You know what I'm talking about.

Danny

Thanks. We'll be all right. Can I keep this? *(He holds up the flashlight.)*

Bellboy

Oh, sure, no problem. Listen, they'll have this fixed before you finish your dinner.

Danny

Come back get the torch, you need it or someone else does.

Bellboy

We got plenty, don't worry. Enjoy your dinner now, folks.

The BELLBOY *leaves, closing the door behind him. The candlelight bathes the room in a warm, rose-colored glow.* DANNY *takes* DIANE'S *hand from her eyes, kisses it, and holds it. She sits still with her eyes closed.*

Danny

You can open 'em, honey. Come on, open up your eyes.

DIANE *opens her eyes, blinks a few times. She looks around without moving her head.*

Diane

It's like being inside a Christmas tree, isn't it? Like sitting on one of the branches, surrounded by ornaments.

Danny *(Laughs.)*

Yeah, yeah. I see what you mean. This is somethin', though, isn't it? We come all the way to New York, the city of lights, and there ain't none. Hold it, maybe that's Paris is the city of lights. But Broadway, anyway. The Great White Way, only now it's black. Or is it London has the Great White Way? Well, let me tell you, sweetheart, when I was out gettin' the Chinese? People are bumpin' into one another, runnin' to get home. Lucky thing I got into the Chinese restaurant when I did, too. Soon as the lights quit, those guys ran and locked the front door. Then they brought out big sheets of plywood and stuck 'em up by the windows. Those Chinese fellas weren't takin' no chances. They were real polite to me, though. Apologized for takin' a little longer than they said was ordinary for my order. Didn't charge me no tax. At least they said they wasn't. Man unlocked the door to let me out, said, You be careful, sir. Hurry, be careful.

Diane

Danny, we're not in China.

Danny

No, honey. New York. We're in New York.

Diane

Why did you speak Chinese to that man?

Danny

What man?

Diane

The doctor who was here before.

Danny

Diane, that was the bellboy. We're going to see the doctor tomorrow, remember? And you know I can't speak Chinese. I barely get by in American.

Diane

Don't be so modest. You know Spanish, too.

Danny

Just about twenty-five words, maybe. Like, *huevos rancheros,* and *buena suerte.*

Diane

Si todo sigue igual.

Danny   *(Laughs.)*

What's that? What's that mean?

Diane

All things being equal. It's an expression. You know what an expression is, Danny. Don't try to fool me.

Danny   *(Hugging her.)*

The last thing I'd ever do is try to fool you, sweetheart. You know I care more for you than anything in the world. There's foolin' around and then there's tryin' to fool. Foolin' around is what we always done best, Di, don't you think? You still like to fool around with your old Danny, don't you? Even after all these years?

Diane

It has been a long time, Danny, hasn't it?

Danny

Almost seventeen years. Since I got out of the service.

DANNY stands up, wipes his forehead, his cheeks. He takes a napkin from the bag and wipes his hands.

Danny

Lord, it's warm. I don't mind the dark, but I could do with some air-coolin'.

He walks over to the windows, which are open. He leans out, trying to catch a breeze. There is none, so he comes back in.

Danny

Could we'd be on Lake Osage this evenin', we were back home. Canoein'. Wouldn't you like that, darlin', if we were lyin' in a canoe lookin' up at the stars, driftin' on Lake Osage?

Diane

Is it a Chinese doctor? The one I'm seeing tomorrow? He's Chinese?

DANNY *comes back over to* DIANE, *kneels in front of her,
taking her hands in his.*

Danny

Diane, listen. Forget this Chinese. The only thing is Chinese is the food that's waitin' for us to eat it in the bag there. The spring rolls and shrimp with lobster sauce and sweet and sour pork and chicken fried rice. All your favorites. The doctor's name is Smith, Hershel Smith. He's a specialist, honey. He'll know what to do. It's all been arranged by the clinic in Tulsa, remember? They said Dr. Smith is the best there is. He's expectin' us tomorrow.

Diane

You were away.

Danny

When, honey? When was I away?

Diane

I'm not sure. You were, though. Away in the Sea of Red.

Danny

The Red Sea. When I was in the navy, you mean?

Diane

Oh, of course. When you said Lake Osage, I thought of it. I took a walk and everything was just like this. There were lights on in the dark, just small ones, shimmering lights.

Danny

Lights on in the houses around the lake.

Diane

I saw you on the other side and I shouted, Danny! Danny! But it wasn't you at all.

DANNY *rests his head on* DIANE'S *lap. She strokes his hair
gently.*

Diane

A fish jumped.

Danny

What kind of fish?

Diane

A Chinese fish.

Danny

How could you tell it was Chinese?

Diane

Because it told my fortune.

Danny

You sure this was at Lake Osage?

Diane

It jumped straight up out of the black water and spoke to me.

Danny

You never told me this before.

Diane

You'd just think I was crazier than I already am. That's why.

Danny

I don't think you're crazy, sweetheart. I don't know what to call it, but it's not crazy. Maybe Dr. Smith has a name for it.

Diane

A fish by any other name is still a fish.

Danny

Even if it's Chinese?

Diane

Definitely if it's Chinese.

Danny

So what did the fish tell you?

Diane

About the children.

Danny *(He is looking up at her now.)*
What about them?

Diane

All about them. Their names, their hair color, the shapes of their noses.

Danny

What children, Diane?

Diane

Ours. Yours and mine, Danny. All of them.

Danny

How many were there?

Diane

Six. Six altogether. Do you really want to know?

Danny

I got no place to go, honey. Not without you, anyway.

Diane

Danny, you were always the sweetest child.

Danny

You didn't meet me until I was twenty, Di. How do you know I was a sweet child?

Diane

You were one of them.

Danny

One of who?

Diane

The six children.

Danny

Wait up. The Chinese fish told you about them?

Diane

You were first, the largest, with red hair and blue eyes.

Danny

Doesn't sound like me.

Diane

The rest were girls. Five perfect girls.

Danny

Did they have red hair and blue eyes, too?

Diane

No. Each one of them had brown hair, brown eyes and brown skin. They looked like fawns.

Danny

You saw them? I thought this was just a fortune the fish told you.

Diane

Danny, these are our children! Don't you recognize them?

Danny   *(Sits next to her again.)*

Di, I love you. *(He kisses her.)* I've loved you since I was twenty and you were eighteen. Seventeen years and I love you more than ever.

Diane

I know, Danny.

Danny

We did have a child. Danny, Junior.

Diane

Dan-Bug.

Danny

That's right, Di. Dan-Bug. We called him Dan-Bug. Do you remember what happened to Dan-Bug, Di?

Diane

Not really.

Danny

Yes, you do. Come on.

Diane

He was two.

Danny

Two years old.

Diane

How old is he now?

Danny

Two. He can't get any older, Di.

Diane

He might have gone in the navy, Danny, like you did.

Danny

He might have.

Diane

I wouldn't have wanted him to go sailing in the Sea of Red. Sailors don't come back from there sometimes.

Danny

I came back, Di. I'm here.

Diane

Dan-Bug's not.

Danny

That's right, Dan-Bug's gone, baby.

Diane

He drowned in the Sea of Red.

Danny

He drowned in Lake Osage.

Diane

The five fawns are fine.

Danny

That's a pretty sentence, Di. The five fawns are fine.

Diane

The Chinese fish was right about them.

Danny

I suppose he ain't half-wrong most of the time.

Diane

I'm dealing with it, Danny. I am. It hasn't been that long.

Danny

Twelve years, Di. How long is long?

Diane

I know this isn't China, Danny. I think I'd like to go there, though.

Danny

That's not impossible. We can see about it. You ready to eat yet?

Diane

Remember Rinky Dink, Dan? What happened to him?

Danny

Yes, Di, I do.

Diane

The woman who was driving never looked in her sideview, she said, just the rearview mirror. Knocked him sideways off his motorcycle into the road in the path of oncoming traffic. Patrolman said Rinky Dink's head hit the ground an instant before that Buick run over his back.

Danny

He was an okay boy, okay.

Diane

He wasn't very big, and he had a three-inch scar on his forehead that filled with red whenever he laughed or was angry. Remember? The car that crushed him didn't leave a mark. There was only a light bruise on his temple that would never heal. When Bonnie saw him in the coffin, she said, Why he looks cuter now than ever.

Danny

When I got out of the navy, before I came back to Oklahoma, I went to visit a guy I'd met in boot camp. We'd kept a correspondence goin', and he was livin' in New Mexico, in the foothills of the Sangre de Cristo range of mountains. His name was Famine McCoy. He reminded me of Rinky Dink. Or Rinky Dink reminded me of him, I forget which.

Anyway, we were ridin' in his truck on some backroad, and we got stuck in a rut. We looked around for some timber, somethin' to get some traction from, but there was nothin' except a petrified stiff dead dog in a ditch on the other side. So we took it and shoved it under the wheel and rocked right out of there. Later we got down to the town and Famine mentioned to a fella he knew what happened and said how he felt a little guilty about abusin' that dog's body and all. Don't worry about it, the guy told him, that's what it's there for. People use it all the time.

Diane

What kind of a name is that, Famine?

Danny

I asked him about it. His real name was Dave, I think. He said that before he went in the navy, he became famous for showin' up on people's doorsteps just at suppertime. Every evenin', he said, he'd go out sniffin'. Just like a dog casin' garbage cans, he'd prowl the neighborhood with his nose up to smell out who was cookin' what. He got to know everybody around where he was livin' and walked the streets until he found a smell he liked, so he knew what they were havin' for dinner. He'd knock on the door, make out like he was just visiting, and don't-mind-if-I-do'd his way to a free meal.

It was his neighbors nicknamed him Famine. They got hip to him and didn't answer their doors until they'd finished eating. Forced him to get a regular job as a carpenter so he could afford to pay for his meals in restaurants. Got himself a hog Lincoln and kept all his tools in it. Told me he didn't have a muffler on it, and he'd drive up and down the streets at suppertime, real slow, gunnin' the motor real loud, so everybody'd know he was out there and that he knew they were eatin', tryin' to make 'em all feel guilty about not invitin' him in anymore.

We wrote to each other for a while after that visit. He told me he lost an eye in some work-related accident and got permanent disability payments from the government and a load of insurance money from the outfit he was carpentryin' for. He moved down to Florida, where he bought himself a piece of land, got married and had a kid or two. He was eatin' steady, I guess. Then I had a letter from his wife, tellin' me Famine was dead.

Seems he was out takin' a dump in the palmettos and felt a sharp jab in his butt. He felt around but couldn't find nothin' wrong, so he just zipped up and didn't think any more about it. That night he started feelin' real bad and actin' strange, so his wife took him to the hospital. The doctor couldn't find anything wrong with him and sent him home. Two hours later, he was dead.

Turned out a snake bit him while he was in the bushes. If he'd told the doctor at the hospital about that jab he'd felt they could have saved him, but it didn't occur to Famine until right before he faded out that it wasn't just a palmetto leaf that stuck him. Poor Famine, just when it looked like things were goin' good, too. Makes me hungry sometimes to think about him.

There is a bright flash in the room, followed by an extremely loud clap of thunder.

Diane

My mother closed the bedroom door.

Danny

What? What door?

Diane

My door. That's what it sounded like when she closed it. Like thunder that's so close. I'd never allow her to put Dan-Bug to bed. I didn't want him to be frightened that way.

Danny

Dan-Bug could sleep through anything, even a thunderstorm. He liked to watch the lightning with me, the double bolts of ground lightning like we get in Oklahoma. Did you know, Di, that a channel of lightning has a width of only about an inch?

DANNY stands up, takes out a handkerchief from his back pocket and wipes the sweat off of his face and neck. He goes over to the window again.

Danny

Too hot to eat, I guess.

DIANE stands and picks up one of the lit candles. She dances around the room, slowly, whirling gracefully. DANNY turns and watches her. She sees that he is watching and she moves gradually in his direction, writhing now, Salome-like, coming closer. Suddenly, the candle she is holding goes out. DIANE stops dancing and stands still for a moment, then her knees buckle and she collapses to the floor. DANNY rushes over and lifts her back onto the couch. She has not lost consciousness, but seems stunned and disoriented. DANNY sits next to her.

Danny

Hey, baby, you all right? Come on, now, talk to me. Talk to me, Di.

Diane *(Very woozy.)*

I am not drunk, Dan. I haven't had a drink since you've been away. Not one. It was Bonnie who made me, wanted me to go out. But I just watched 'em. Cranberry juice and soda water, that's all I had. We were at the Cherokee and there was a good band. Played a lot of old stuff, made me cry 'cause you were away. I was sittin' on the toilet after I peed, cryin' 'cause I missed you, and Bonnie was in there with Rinky Dink doin' lines. They offered me some but you know me and drugs is not on friendly terms, so I declined. All it took was that woman's small miscalculation and Rink was dust.

Danny

I wasn't anywhere, Di. I wasn't away.

Diane

Oh, you were, you were. Off sailing in the Sea of Red. Do you know how it hurts your eyes to stare at the horizon? If you stare at the horizon for too long all you can see is fire. The entire line of the horizon is burning. Fires as far as the eyes can see.

Danny

Come back, Diane. I'm here, it's okay. You don't have to pretend now.

Diane

Danny, Danny. Can you keep a secret?

Danny

Sure.

Diane

When we go to see this doctor—what's his name?

Danny

Dr. Smith, you mean? Hershel Smith?

Diane

When we go to see Dr. Smith. Don't tell him about Dan-Bug, okay? Can we forget about Dan-Bug?

Danny

I think Dr. Smith already knows about Dan-Bug, sweetheart. He's spoken to the people at the Tulsa clinic. They sent your medical records to him. That's how come he agreed to see you, see what he could do. I told you that, honey. I told you before we left home.

Diane

Gee, Danny, it's so dark here. It's so hot, and there isn't any moon.

Danny

There's a power failure, Di. The lights are out all over New York City. AC's out, too. At least in this hotel they got windows can open. Some places they're sealed shut.

Diane

It's kind of beautiful, though, the dark. Don't you think, Dan? I could get used to this.

> *The telephone rings so loudly that it startles both* DANNY *and* DIANE. DANNY *is about to pick up the receiver but it does not ring a second time. He waits, staring at the phone, but nothing happens.*

Danny

Now that's spooky.

Diane

Spooky?

Danny

The telephone. It rang once, then quit.

Diane

Maybe it was a signal.

Danny

What kind of a signal?

Diane

A message.

Danny

Nobody knows we're here, Di. I mean, nobody knows what hotel we're staying at. I didn't tell anyone. Somebody rang the wrong room, that's all.

The telephone rings again. DANNY *looks at it and lets it ring a second time, then a third. After the fourth ring, he picks it up.*

Danny

Hello?

He listens for a few moments, starts to speak, then stops and listens again. DANNY *hangs up. A few moments pass in silence. The telephone rings again. On the second ring,* DANNY *picks it up.*

Danny

Hello?

DANNY *listens for a moment, then hands the receiver to* DIANE, *who looks at him but does not talk into the phone.*

Diane

Who is it?

Danny

He asked for you.

Diane   *(Lifts the receiver to her ear and mouth.)*

Hello? Yes, yes it is. Thank you. It is dark, yes, very dark. We have candles. Uh huh. I'm sure it's not. No, I never have. Yes, Danny went out and got Chinese. You're very kind. I hope so. Yes. Yes. Thank you. We will. Bye.

DIANE *hands the receiver to* DANNY *and he hangs it up.*

Danny

Who was it?

Diane

Dr. Smith. He was very sweet.

Danny

The clinic must have told him where we were staying. What did he say?

Diane

He just wanted to make sure that we were all right during the blackout. That we were comfortable and had food.

Danny

That must have been him the first time, too. When the line was messed up. Someone was talking but I couldn't understand him. The connection was bad, full of static.

Diane

He wanted to assure me, he said, that he was looking forward to our visit tomorrow. He has a nice voice, Danny, you know? A *good* voice.

Danny

I'm glad.

Diane

I'm going to tell him about Dan-Bug.

Danny

I know, Di. You have to.

Diane

I couldn't live without you, Danny. I really couldn't.

> DIANE *puts her head on* DANNY'S *shoulder. His arm embraces her.*

Danny

Jesus, honey, you're burnin' up.

> DANNY *gets up and goes into the bathroom. He comes out with a wet washcloth, sits down next to* DIANE, *and uses it to wipe perspiration from her face. Then he folds it and presses it against her forehead.*

Diane

Danny, I didn't tell you everything about the fawns.

Danny

The fawns?

Diane

You know, the five fawns.

Danny *(Removes the washcloth and wipes his own face with it.)*

What about the fawns, honey?

Diane

They have names.

Danny

Did you name them?

Diane

Of course. Don't pretend you don't know.

Danny *(Laughs.)*

Me? I ain't pretendin', sweetheart. What are they?

Diane

Thumb, Index, Middle, Third and Pinkie. Pinkie's my favorite.

Danny

Diane, you're the one and only, that's for sure.

Diane

Dan-Bug drowned, didn't he, Danny?

Danny

Yes, honey, he did.

Diane

Do you recall how it happened?

Danny

You and me was makin' love down on the shore of Lake Osage. We thought the boy was asleep on his blanket, but he woke up and walked into the water without makin' no noise we could hear. By the time we found him, he was gone.

Diane

It was a long time ago, Danny.

Danny

Twelve years, Di, like I said. Not so long. It's good you can talk about it, though. If you didn't, I'd probably lose you, too.

Diane

Me and the five fawns, you mean.

Danny

Yeah. Them, also.

Diane

That night I was in the Cherokee, the night Rinky Dink was killed, Bonnie said somethin'.

Danny

What was that?

Diane

Oh, she was wasted, I guess. But I heard her say to Peggy Worth how it was some people don't deserve to have kids, anyway.

Danny

And you figured she was meanin' you?

Diane

Uh huh. I didn't take it to heart right away, but then after it turned out I couldn't get pregnant again, I started in on it meanin' somethin'. There was no way I could get it out of my head. It just stuck in my brain like a knife. It got so bad that I asked 'em at the Tulsa clinic could they just do an operation pull out that knife.

Danny

It ain't been easy on me, neither, Di. You driftin' in and out, though, I suppose give me a purpose in life since the accident. Needed to keep you from gettin' away from yourself altogether.

Diane

Driftin' so far out into the Sea of Red I couldn't get back, you mean.

Danny　*(Looking at her.)*

I have to admit there been times lately I been feelin' a little desperate. I'm a pretty good hand, they tell me, but it comes to bakin' cakes I'm clutterin' up the kitchen. It's a damn hard thing to take, feelin' useless.

Diane

You don't have a useless bone in your body, Danny. I'll tell everyone we know.

Danny　*(Moves closer to her.)*

If it weren't so damn hot, I'd kiss you.

Diane

Kiss me anyway.

As they kiss, the lights suddenly go on in the room, as does the air-conditioning. DANNY *gets up and goes to the window.*

Danny

Look at this, Di. The whole city's lit up!

DIANE *joins him at the window and they stare at the magnificent sight. They embrace and kiss tenderly.*

Danny

Honey, what would you say to some Chinese food?

Fade Out.

END

MRS. KASHFI

Characters

CHARLIE, *a boy of eight*

THE MOTHER, *a woman of thirty*

MRS. KASHFI, *an old woman*

MR. DE WITT, *a man approaching middle age*

ROSE, *a woman in her fifties*

A DESK CLERK AT THE HOTEL

A BELLHOP

SETTING: *lobby and rooms of a hotel in a big city, 1952*

THE LOBBY OF THE HOTEL

We see a man, whom we will later come to know as MR.
DE WITT, *registering at the desk.* MR. DE WITT, *having
completed his registration, follows a bellhop, who carries* MR.
DE WITT'S *suitcase and a room key, to the elevator. They go
up.*

Just after MR. DE WITT *goes into the elevator, we see
a boy, about eight years old, and his mother, a beautiful
woman of thirty or so, enter the hotel. The boy hurries along
behind his mother as they walk toward the elevator.*

*We next see the woman and the boy disembarking from
the elevator on a floor of the hotel. She hustles the boy along the
corridor to the appropriate room. She straightens her clothing
and the boy's before knocking on the door.*

*The hotel's carpet is worn, the furnishings shabby. A cou-
ple of bulbs in the corridor are burnt out. The hotel has seen
better days, so the presence of this classy-looking, slightly over-
dressed woman is somewhat jarring, given the circumstance of
the surroundings. The woman seems oblivious to the conditions,
however.*

*A wizened old woman opens the door of the room. She is
wearing several sweaters, a shawl, and some kind of headwrap.
Small and bent, she has a large nose and wears pince-nez on a
chain around her neck.*

Mother

We're a little early, Mrs. Kashfi, I know. I hope it's all right.

Mrs. Kashfi

Of course, my dear. Please come in. And this is your son?

MRS. KASHFI'S APARTMENT

The boy and his mother enter the hotel apartment of MRS.
KASHFI, *which is stifling, terribly overheated, belying the old
lady's appearance. The boy begins reacting immediately, sweat-*

ing, wiping his face. His mother, however, pays no attention to the temperature. She is focused, single-minded, purposeful in the extreme.

Mother

Yes, today is his birthday. He's eight years old. We're going to the toy store later.

Mrs. Kashfi   *(to boy)*

What a lovely child, so big and handsome. May I get you some candy? Do you like chocolate?

> *Without waiting for his reply,* MRS. KASHFI *shuffles over to a table, the surface of which is crowded with objects, as is every part of the front room of her apartment: old photos in ornate frames, bizarre bric-a-brac. She picks up a cut-glass dish filled with half-melted dark brown shapes: the chocolates. She presents it to the boy, who is gazing around the room, half-fascinated, half-horrified. He studies the dirty walls, worn overstuffed chairs and sofas, a variety of religious objects, dirt-smeared windows, and, the centerpiece, a large birdcage on a stand that contains a single inhabitant: a fat, dinge-yellow parakeet.*
>
> *The boy recoils at the sight of the proffered candy, and refuses by shaking his head, keeping silent, turning away from the melting mess. He walks over to the birdcage.*

Mrs. Kashfi   *(talking to the parakeet)*

Say hello, Nostradamus. You have a visitor. *(To boy)* Nostradamus is blind, but he has an ancient soul that enables him to see through time. *(Turns to* MOTHER*)* Are you ready now, dear? Nostradamus will keep your lovely boy company.

Boy

Where are you going, Mommy?

Mrs. Kashfi

She's going on a voyage. We'll be sailing on the sea of clairvoyance.

Mother   *(to boy)*

I won't be very long, Charlie. Wait out here for me. *(To* MRS. KASHFI, *as they walk toward another room)* Yes, Mrs. Kashfi, it's my mother. She died last month and I need to know a few things. I must know if she's all right.

Mrs. Kashfi   *(as they enter the other room)*

What is your mother's name, dear?

Mother

Rose.

> *The door to the other room closes on* MRS. KASHFI *and the boy's mother, leaving the boy alone in the outer room.*
>
> *We see the lobby of the hotel. The man who entered the hotel and registered before the boy and his mother came in,* MR. DE WITT, *gets off the elevator and walks over to the desk.*

Mr. De Witt   *(to* DESK CLERK*)*

Excuse me, I am Mr. De Witt, in number 35. I have no memory at all. If you please, each time I come in, I'll tell you my name and each time you'll tell me the number of my room. Please keep the key or I'm afraid I'll lose it.

> *He places the room key on the counter.*

Desk Clerk

Very well, sir.

Mr. De Witt   *leaves the hotel.*

> *The outer room of* MRS. KASHFI'S *apartment. The boy circumnavigates the room. It is hellishly hot, and he unbuttons his coat. He goes to the window, rubs the glass with his elbow, with the palms of his hands, smearing the dirt further, and can see only the bricks of another building. The parakeet is dropping feces steadily onto the floor of its cage. We hear a steady "tup, tup" sound emanating from the birdcage. The place smells bad, and the boy winces, holding his nose.*

He finally sits down on a lumpy couch. Murmuring can be heard from the inner room. The boy sits and waits, involuntarily listening to the parakeet's evacuation, the sound of which is quite loud. The boy tries holding his breath, then exhaling hard; takes in a sharp breath and holds it. He glances at the window and sees in it a reflection of a woman, her face not quite discernible. The boy turns his gaze to the center of the room and sees his grandmother, ROSE, standing there next to the birdcage. She is wearing a white satin robe and is very carefully groomed. She is as beautiful as the boy's mother, her daughter.

Rose
Hello, Charlie.

Charlie
Nanny! Mommy said you were dead!

Rose   *(smiling. She is very gentle with her grandson.)*
Everyone dies, Charlie. But that doesn't mean they're gone.

The boy gets off the couch and goes to ROSE, *who bends and kisses him.*

Charlie
Nanny, you're real, it's really you! Let's go tell Mommy!

Rose
No, Charlie. I've come just to see you.

Charlie
But Nanny, Mommy's in the other room with that old lady fortune-teller, Mrs. Kashfi. Mommy wants to know what happened to you.

Rose
The woman will tell your mother what she wants to hear. Your mother only hears what she wants to, anyway. Mrs. Kashfi knows this.

Charlie

Do you know the fortune-teller, Nanny?

Rose

No.

Charlie

Then how does she know what to say to Mommy?

Rose

Mrs. Kashfi will read what is written on your mother's face.

Charlie

Gee, Nanny, I've never seen any writing on Mommy's face. You mean, like tattoos?

Rose (taking CHARLIE'S *hand and guiding him back to the couch, where they sit down together*)

Charlie, your mother is upset, she's very unhappy.

Charlie

I know, because you died.

Rose

Well, yes, partly because of that. You see, I died without having told her about something. Charlie, you're old enough to know about money, aren't you?

Charlie

Sure. You need money to buy things. Mommy said she'd take me to the toy store after she's finished with Mrs. Kashfi. It's my birthday!

Rose

Of course, Charlie. I know today is your birthday. And I have a present for you.

Charlie

Wow, Nanny, I didn't know people could give presents after they're dead.

Rose

Charlie, listen carefully. Your mother loves you, but she is a very selfish woman. Do you remember all of the time we spent together?

Charlie

Yeah, when Mommy was away. She was away a lot.

Rose

Yes, Charlie. I enjoyed taking care of you, but it was difficult for me. I had a bad heart, and your mother knew this. But she left you with me, anyway.

Charlie

She brought me lots of presents when she came back from her trips.

Rose

Yes, of course she did. And eight years ago she brought me a wonderful gift.

Charlie

What was it, Nanny?

Rose

A little boy named Charlie.

Charlie

Me! It was me!

Rose

That's right, Charlie, it was you. The greatest gift I ever received.

Charlie

Nanny, did you know my daddy?

Rose

No, sweetheart, I don't know who your daddy is.

Charlie

Didn't Mommy tell you?

Rose

I don't think she knows who he is, either. She never told me his name. Your mother has her own way of doing things, Charlie, and there's not much anybody can do about that. She never would listen to me.

Charlie

Where's my gift, Grandma?

Rose

Can you keep a secret?

Charlie *(nodding)*

Yes, Grandma.

Rose

There is a key taped to the bottom of your toy chest.

Charlie

Who put it there?

Rose

I did.

Charlie

Why?

Rose

So your mother would not find it.

Charlie

What's the key to?

Rose

Your future, Charlie. That's why you must not tell her about it.

They hear laughter from the inner room.

Rose

Charlie, the key is to a box at the bank. You know the big gray building I used to take you to?

Charlie

You made me sit on that hard bench and wait for you. Then after you'd buy me ice cream.

Rose

That's right, Charlie. Listen carefully: Inside the box is a letter addressed to an officer of the bank, Mr. De Witt. You've never met him but he's very nice. As soon as you can, I want you to take the key and go to the bank and ask to see Mr. De Witt. Tell him I told you to have him open the box and read the letter inside. You'll be taken care of, Charlie, and you will never have to depend on your mother. Remember, Charlie, don't tell her about any of this. Tell her you're going out to play and then get the key and walk over to the bank. Do you remember how to get there?

Charlie   *(nods)*

Yes, Nanny.

Rose

If Mr. De Witt isn't there, either wait for him or go back another time. Hide the key under the toy chest again if you have to. But your mother must not know about this. Do you understand?

Charlie

I guess so, Nanny. But why can't I tell Mommy?

Rose

If you do, Charlie, you'll never receive your birthday present from me. I intended to take care of this myself, but before I could, I died. Mr. De Witt will have to do it for me.

Charlie

You were in bed for a long time, Nanny.

Rose

Yes, Charlie, too long a time. We never did have that dance

we'd planned on. Come, Charlie, come dance with me now.

Charlie
I'm not such a good dancer, Grandma. And there isn't any music.

She stands and pulls him up with her, holding his arms. Dancing partners.

Rose
Of course, you are. And of course there's music. Just listen!

We hear a sweet, plaintive tone, to which CHARLIE *and his grandmother begin twirling around the room, circling the birdcage. Nostradamus, the parakeet, twitters away for the first time, brought to life by the music.*

Charlie
Gee, Nanny, I'm dancing pretty good, huh?

Rose
Magnificently, Charlie! You're a marvelous dancer. Remember that all women love to dance, Charlie. It transports them.

Charlie
I never knew you could do this, Nanny. You were always so sick.

Rose
Oh, I loved to dance when I was young. I danced every chance I had.

Charlie
Tell me about when you were a girl, Grandma. What were you like then?

Rose *(laughs at the question and the memories)*
I was a little wild, I guess. Not the same as your mother, but I enjoyed life. My father, your great-grandfather, played

the violin in an orchestra. He taught me to dance. I remember when I was just a bit older than you are now, my parents wouldn't allow me to wear any makeup, so I'd spit on a red woolen blanket and rub it on my cheeks. One day I made a date with my sister's boyfriend. I borrowed one of her dresses and snuck out of the house to meet him, and who did I run into but my sister! Your great-aunt Lily. She made me take off her dress right on the street! Lily, poor thing, she never forgave me for that.

They stop dancing and stand together, holding hands.

Rose

Oh, Charlie, I did everything when I was young. I ice-skated, roller-skated. I was a champion high-diver. I loved to swim and ride horses and run. I was a great runner! I'm so sorry I could never run with you.

Charlie

When did you get sick?

Rose

After your mother was born. They called it "brain fever" but it was really an infection of the heart, and I was never the same after that. I couldn't do the things I used to, the things I loved. I always had to rest, to stay in bed and rest.

Charlie

What about Grandpa?

Rose

He got bored, I suppose. I was no fun any more, always sick, so he left. Went away, and that was the end of that. I don't really blame him, I was never angry about his leaving. I don't know why I wasn't, it's just the way I am. Or was, I should say, when I was alive.

Charlie

After you died I was with Mommy in her bedroom at night and a giant golden moth appeared at the window and banged itself against the glass. It wouldn't go away and kept banging its body against the glass. Mommy got scared and turned off the light. She said there couldn't be a big moth like that flying around outside in the middle of the winter, that it had to be your spirit, Nanny, coming to visit us. It frightened me, too. Mommy made us sit still in the dark for a long time, and when she turned the light on again the moth was gone. Was it, Nanny? Was it your spirit?

Before ROSE *can answer, we hear noise from the inner room, the voices of* CHARLIE'S *mother and* MRS. KASHFI.

Rose
Charlie, remember about the key. Don't say anything to your mother and take it to Mr. De Witt. Do as I've told you. I have to go now. I love you, Charlie. You're a big boy now.

She kisses him.
We see the hotel lobby. MR. DE WITT *enters the hotel and goes to the desk.*

Mr. De Witt
I'm Mr. De Witt. May I have my key, please?

Desk Clerk   *(handing him a key)*
Number 35, sir.

Mr. De Witt   *(taking the key)*
Thank you.

He heads for the elevator.
We see the door of MRS. KASHFI'S *inner room open. Out come* MRS. KASHFI *and the boy's mother, their faces serene and aglow. They find* CHARLIE *alone in the front room. The mother is holding a teacup.*

Mother
Look, Charlie, look at this.

She goes to him and shows him the contents of the cup. CHAR-

LIE *stares into it, as do we. There are a few brown bits gathered in the bottom, tea leaves. The evidence on which* MRS. KASHFI *bases her "reading."*

Charlie *(looking back up at his mother)*
What does it mean?

Mother
Your grandmother is safe and happy.

Charlie
I know, she was just here.

MRS. KASHFI *and the boy's mother look at each other and laugh gently, amused by* CHARLIE'S *remark and obviously self-satisfied.*

Mother
Thank you, Mrs. Kashfi.

The mother hands the teacup back to MRS. KASHFI, *then opens her purse and takes out some bills, which she also gives to the old woman.* MRS. KASHFI *folds the bills and sticks them in a pocket of one of her sweaters.*

Mother
I hope that's the right amount.

Mrs. Kashfi
I'm sure it is, dear.

Mother
I'll see you next week. Time to go, Charlie.

They head for the door to the corridor.

Mrs. Kashfi
Did you have a nice time with Nostradamus, Charlie?

Charlie
Yes, ma'am. He sang while we danced.

Mrs. Kashfi

You danced? With whom?

Charlie

Nanny. I danced with Nanny.

> MRS. KASHFI *and the mother laugh again. Now* CHARLIE *and his mother exit, as* MRS. KASHFI *holds open the door.*

Mrs. Kashfi

See you next week.

> *The elevator door opens to the lobby and* CHARLIE *and his mother walk out of the hotel. Coming in through the revolving door as they leave is* MR. DE WITT, *but he is barely recognizable. He is extraordinarily upset. His clothes are torn, he is covered with dirt and mud, and his face is a bloody mess. He staggers over to the desk and addresses the astonished clerk.*

Mr. De Witt

De Witt, I'm Mr. De Witt.

Desk Clerk

What do you mean, you're Mr. De Witt? Mr. De Witt has just gone upstairs!

Mr. De Witt

I'm sorry, it's me . . . I've just fallen out of the window. Please, what's the number of my room?

Fade Out.

END

Barry Gifford was born on October 18, 1946, in Chicago, Illinois, and raised there and in Key West and Tampa, Florida. He has received awards from PEN, the National Endowment for the Arts, the Art Directors Club of New York and the American Library Association. His writing has appeared in *Punch, Esquire, Cosmopolitan, Rolling Stone, Sport,* the *New York Times,* the *New York Times Book Review* and many other publications. Mr. Gifford's books have been translated into fifteen languages, and his novel *Wild at Heart* was made into an award-winning film. His book *Night People* was awarded the Premio Brancati, the Italian National Book Award established by Pier Paolo Pasolini and Alberto Moravia. Mr. Gifford has written screenplays for the film version of his own *Perdita Durango,* and for Francis Ford Coppola's production of Jack Kerouac's *On the Road.* He lives in the San Francisco Bay Area.

BOOKS BY BARRY GIFFORD

FICTION

Baby Cat-Face
Arise and Walk
Night People
The Sailor and Lula Novels:
    Wild at Heart
    Perdita Durango
    Sailor's Holiday
    Sultans of Africa
    Consuelo's Kiss
    Bad Day for the Leopard Man
A Good Man to Know
New Mysteries of Paris
Port Tropique
An Unfortunate Woman
Landscape with Traveler
A Boy's Novel

NONFICTION

A Day at the Races: The Education of a Racetracker
The Devil Thumbs a Ride and Other Unforgettable Films
The Neighborhood of Baseball
Saroyan: A Biography (with Lawrence Lee)
Jack's Book: An Oral Biography of Jack Kerouac (with
    Lawrence Lee)

POETRY

Ghosts No Horse Can Carry: Collected Poems 1967–1987
Giotto's Circle
Beautiful Phantoms: Selected Poems
Persimmons: Poems for Paintings
The Boy You Have Always Loved
Poems from Snail Hut
Horse hauling timber out of Hokkaido forest
Coyote Tantras
The Blood of the Parade

PLAYS

Hotel Room Trilogy

TRANSLATIONS

Selected Poems of Francis Jammes (with Bettina Dickie)